FINDING IT: Your One Week Guide Toward Job Seeking Success

By O. Michele Giacomini

WHO WANTS A FREEBIE???

Learn my Top Favorite 5 Tips for Success

Go to this link here today:

http://bit.ly/5SuccessTips

DEDICATION

This book is dedicated to my amazing sons, Eric & Ryan.
Without you, none of this matters. The two of you have
been able to put career seeking opportunities into place,
and you did it without having "hover parents" finding the
jobs for you. BRAVO!!!

Thank you both for always inspiring me
to learn, to grow, to be open to life's new adventures.
Always.

I would also like to acknowledge some dear friends who
were either supports or inspirations for writing this book.
They are the people in my life who take life's lemons and
make the best dang lemonade outta them you can
imagine!
Dave, Sandy, Susan, Deanna, Chris, Steve, and Matt.

Let our knowledge help lift others to success, so that we
may continue making a positive difference in this world.

<u>CONTENTS</u>

Acknowledgements i

Chapter 1:
How the Hell do I do this?

Chapter 2:
They Said

Chapter 3:
Get your Butt out of Bed and Get Going

Chapter 4:
DAY 1: How to get Started when I can Barely Start Myself?

Chapter 5:
DAY 2: Seize the Day!

Chapter 6:
DAY 3: Oh My Gawd, how will I Pay my Bills?

Chapter 7:
Day 4: Let's get Resourceful

Chapter 8:
Day 5: Out of the Box Thinking

Chapter 9:
Now What?

Chapter 10:
Your Loved Ones Need Support too!

ACKNOWLEDGMENTS

The nature of this book is to help lift others upward and onward with strategies to assist them with job seeking. All names in this book (besides the dedication and my own) have been changed to protect the identity of the people whose stories have been shared. This book, (and its companion pieces), in no way guarantees job placement.

IMPORTANT: This book has been set up to be a step by step guide on how to use the program. Simply read and do the exercises as laid out and you should be able to kick some major butt by the end of the week on your job search skills and routine!

TO BEGIN:

Take a moment to read the first two chapters of the <u>Finding It Guidebook</u>. Don't let that freak you out. They are super short and will give you the background information on this program so that you may understand whys and the how of using this program. Plus, they help you pre-plan for Day 1. Trust the process!

AUTHOR'S NOTE:

I highly recommend using this guidebook with the <u>Finding It: The Video</u> (companion piece). It serves to help you more insight on the practice of this book and the important of frontloading, etc. in order to organize your action plan for success.

"The secret to getting ahead is getting started."
~Mark Twain

Chapter 1
How the Hell do I do this?

When I graduated from high school, I knew what I wanted to do, but that was not going to happen. I just didn't have the support system, nor the "in" with people who could help me become the world's great actor. I was already taking college courses in the afternoon, so college was definitely my next option. So I had to soul search on what the hell I was going to do with my life, that would use my natural talents and abilities. So after some deep reflection, I realized I could use my speaking abilities, my ease on camera and my love for writing and become a television reporter. And that is exactly what I set out to do for the next four or five years.

What I didn't expect was to meet the absolute love of my life and allow his dreams of staying put in Northern California derail my dreams. Do I regret that? Yes, and no! I have had my moments where I got real pissed at myself for not following my dreams...but the truth is, I believe he was put in my path of success to guide me in a different direction. Truly. So long story short, I ended up working in print journalism (yes, there really was such a thing back in the early days when the earth was cooling). This lead me to a career as a magazine editor at a VERY young age, when magazines were not found on-line, (or at least not many) and by staying in touch with my television news friends, they encouraged me to use my go-getter personality to go into Public Relations. I did. And I ran a very successful PR business for eight years, until I got bit by the teaching bug and transitioned into education, only to find myself some 17 years later, in a high position in the ed. world, longing to get back to my writing and public relations days. So I did...on the side. My side hustle.

So at this point you may wonder why I am sharing this with you, right?

Let's face it, college is NOT for everyone.

Trade schools are beginning to turn out some of the highest paid workers these days.

Many younger folks have watched the crap & stress their parents went through trying to get ahead and climb the corporate ladder, or just get a freaking foot on the damn ladder.

Some do not want to live a life like their parents which was/is heavily imbalanced with work/life--work being the vast majority of where they spend their time.

Many are more minimalistic in attitude, so big money is not necessarily the goal, and job satisfaction and life experiences are more key.

And let's face it, some of you may/may not want to admit you have had your parents hovering over you protecting you your whole life, and you are ready to get out there and stand on your own. (Some of you may not have had parents doing this, but you too want to get out there and conquer the world on your own).

Problem is, you may not know quite how to do that.

So I shared my journey with you to show you that life is nuts, and can lead you in all sorts of directions and sometimes back full circle. Regardless, it is an adventure. Finding a job is a career adventure, and that is the way you need to think of it...very positive! YOU CAN DO THIS! And you will, but YOU need to put in the effort. You will only get out of this what you put in, so keep that in mind.

I am not here to hover over you and do everything for you. It may seem like that a bit at first, but what this guidebook will do is help teach you how to get yourself set up for success, so that you can do this on your own. Will you need help along the way? Yes, but it will all make more sense when you work through the program.

This guide is about navigating the path to your next (or first) career adventure. It's not a know-it-all-tell-all book, it's a let-me-help-you-get-off-your-butt-and-get-going literary tool.

At times you are going to discover that life isn't always fair. But you are going to grab life's crappy lemons and squeeze them so hard you make the best darn lemonade of your life! So, that said, let's go over this guidebook and how to use it, because understanding what this tool is about, is key:

- This guide serves to communicate a system about helping you to help yourself get it together and get moving on finding either your first or another job. (You have competition out there, so there is not a second to lose)!

- This guide is about showing you many of the components that are important parts of the job search process and how to assimilate them into a working daily schedule, so that you may have the structure to look for resources, leads and ultimately a new job. Keep in mind that everyone is different, so you will need to customize this structure to fit your lifestyle—but also remember that for now, finding your first/next job IS your job, so make it a priority, as you would any job!

- This guide is for writing in, making notes, brainstorming, you name it. So go ahead, mark it up, notate, dog-ear, whatever you need. USE IT! Besides, the worse it looks by the time you find your next job or career, just means you have used the heck out of it...so go for it!
(AUTHOR'S NOTE: This is also why you will see the extra margin spacing in the print version—intentionally done so you can make notes in the margins or wherever you want. You're welcome)!

- This guide is big on helping you organize and structure your day. Essentially, you are starting a job of finding a job, and there's a lot to it...and for many people, it is a LOT to learn, real fast.

- This guide is a bit overwhelming AT FIRST, but as you get your routine going and start using all the parts and pieces, it all starts to make sense, and in the long run you will make so much more headway, as a result. The first day of Prep and Day 1 are the hardest, then it is a cakewalk from there on out. You will need to read Chapters 1-4 first, (then you will read one chapter per night for the following chapters, so that you are prepared for what will happen the next day). For the best results, I recommend reading Chapters 1 & 2, then completing the exercises that go with those chapters, then read Chapter 3 and do its exercises, then read Chapter 4 so that you are prepared for all that will actually happen on Day 1. (I realize some of you are chomping at the bit to get going, and that is okay, if you have the time to dedicate today. If not, just follow the suggested reading & exercises/lessons for today of Chapters 1-4, no worries, they are super short chapters). Besides, you may want to have a little lead time to find your office supplies, notebooks, etc that you will need to be ready to hit the ground running on your official Day 1.

  Simply put, if you just start reading through the book and taking care of the exercises/lessons as they pop up, you will be doing great!

- After you complete the tasks for Day 1, please read Chapter 5 that evening, to be ready for Day 2 the next day, and so on. We call that "frontloading" in the education/professional development world. It helps you to be prepared for what is coming next. (Try not to read further ahead than that. That's not because of any big surprises lurking later in the book, it's simply so you do not overwhelm yourself more. You are going through a lot. Take a beat and trust this process—it will be enough to digest daily, besides trying to take it all in at once)! I also recommend that if you have loved ones all over your case about finding a job and getting out there, ask them to read the last chapter of this book so they see what you are going through and how you are using this program--I believe if you do, most of the time they will get the bigger picture and get on the "Support & Cheer You On Bandwagon" quickly.

- And remember, this guide is also about viewing finding a new job as adventure. Make it fun and exciting everyday!

*"Don't listen to what people say.
Watch what they do."*
~Author unknown

Chapter 2
THEY SAID

When I started out trying to seek my first career, people reassured me that I I had what it took and it would happened. They told me I would also need to pay my dues and be stronger for it.

Well let's get REAL honest about that. I am NOT so thankful about the DUES paying part. It sucked. Yes, I've learned some things about myself I wouldn't have, had this not happened—but I am not exactly doing cartwheels of gratitude for that super long period of my life. What I found is that this Type A constantly-on-the-go personality was suddenly dealing with painstakingly slow processes. It's true. I wanted to be the best and on top leading the charge, immediately.

"They" said a lot of things…but there was even more that "they" didn't say.

They didn't say it would take me months and months, (years actually), to work my way up. They didn't say I would begin to understand why so many of my friends would give up on their dreams and just go find jobs to get them by. They didn't say I'd constantly question each and every career move I'd ever make. They didn't say I would be so nervous once I landed my first (and following) career job(s) that I would be paranoid for months to be "myself" for fear my new employer would think I wasn't good enough. They didn't say that sometimes I would screw up and take a job in hell-hole.

Those aren't fun things, so "they" didn't say anything about that stuff, they just kept referring to "Pay your dues." But I am speaking up.

I want you to know what I discovered through my flippin' job seeking adventures...because it was NOT all rosy and wonderful all the time, and I don't want you to think that something is wrong because you aren't feeling chipper about the whole process. First, it is very normal to feel all of those not-so-fun things and more. You are NOT alone. And if you begin to feel depressed, get help from family, friends and medical professionals. Tell people you are depressed about this situation. (Yes, they probably already know, but there is something about finally vocalizing it, that begins to help lift the weight of depression off your shoulders). So enlist help with dealing with this part—-remember you are moving on to some kinda "scary" but exciting unknowns and you don't have a crystal ball, so it is okay to get down, but be sure to find someone to talk to about this, especially if you are finding yourself more down than up!

Here are some tips on how I got through the down times (keep in mind that everyone is different, so you need to determine what will help you best if you are experiencing depression—and I am NOT a medical doctor, nor a mental health professional, so if you are experiencing depression, be sure to contact one immediately).

- I was fortunate to be able to contact a psychologist through Employee Assistance. If you do not have this through yourself, a parent/guardian, or a spouse, ask your medical practitioner to guide you. You might also contact your local Health Department and ask about local resources you may contact to discuss your depression. Also, there are national resource hotlines to help people who need emotional assistance, such as: https://suicidepreventionlifeline.org/talk-to-someone-now/
Just do NOT delay if you need help—get the help, and get it fast!

- Weight began to lift once I finally admitted to my significant other that I was battling depression. (I wish I would have admitted it immediately to someone, anyone, instead of trying to hide it, because it would have helped me move forward faster).

- I developed a daily "work" routine. Finding work became my new job. Making a list of my daily accomplishments lifted my spirits greatly! (Made me feel like a total badass at the end of each day, quite frankly)!

- I started reading every business success book I could get my hands on. (Later on, I started looking for podcast interviews/YouTube Videos with very successful people).

- I started a slideshow of positive memes I came across, a collection of positivity, if you will. Everyday I watched it and added to it as I discovered more. Occasionally, I wrote down my positives and my gratitudes (this was something I now know I should have done more of, to move forward faster). I also created a playlist of empowerment songs. I call it my "Pump Me Up Playlist," and add songs that make me feel confidant, strong and bad-frickin'-ass.

- I reached out to friends I could trust to talk to about my feelings and fears. I was selective on who I shared this information with, and they became a super inner circle of support through this difficult time.

- I listed, listed and listed some more all the things, traits, etc. that I am good at.

- I also listened to the positives "they" said and was realistic that I would also need to deal with the stuff "they" weren't saying while I kicked ass to find a my job. (Aka: Perspective).

(Take a moment to notice that there are a LOT of "I" statements in that list, as well as throughout this book. Why? Because I took accountability for myself and my actions. I am the one who dug myself out of the pit of despair. Did I have help here and there along the way? You bet! But I am the one who chose to put one foot in front of the other, every single freaking day, and kept myself in motion, while I navigated the fog that was trying to envelope me. Because of this, I was able to move forward and into the clear skies of clarity more quickly than my friends and former coworkers who have chosen the route of wallowing in self-pity.)

I believe that you are choosing to also move forward, and propel yourself onward and upward. Soon these "I statements" will be your "I statements," customized for you, of course! That's why you are reading this book right now! Because you are making a positive choice to move forward and reach your goals of attaining your next/first job! Way to go! You've made the first big step. Good for you!

These are techniques I encourage you to customize and engage in. But the most important is getting help, and finding someone to talk to about the depression, if you are experiencing it. If you aren't, well, good for you, that is truly awesome and I mean that with heartfelt sincerity—but the reality is, many people do become disheartened by this sort of new and important life event, and the level can vary from person to person. You really can work through those feelings as you launch yourself forward to finding a new job. So, point being, if you feel depressed, please pause this book for a moment and find help immediately. Then check that off your To Do List, and get back to the book!

JD

I noticed when working with JD he was doing a great job of "holding it together" emotionally with his new adventure of seeking a new career. Considering others I have counselled, I thought he was rather stoic and wanted to understand more about how he was remaining poised.

He shared with me that he had his moments when it was tough, but for the most part, because he had dived in immediately with the Finding It program, he didn't have time to dwell on the negativity or rejections that came his way on occasion. His daily accomplishments were keeping his spirits high. Plus, by discussing his situation with trusted friends and acquaintances, their feedback was bolstering his confidence & belief that career

---

adventure was right around the corner, and he knew he had people keeping him in mind for potential leads.

Most of all, JD also confided that his discussions with those he knew who had gone through something similar, helped him see he was not alone in this unexpected & unplanned for journey.

LESSON: DAY 1-WHAT IS YOUR WHY?

After read Chapters **Chapters 1 & 2** of the guidebook, respond to the following:

What is your "WHY"?

Take a moment to think about your "WHY."   Why are you looking for a new job? I know that may seem obvious, but it isn't necessarily. I am asking you to drill down and get to the root of why you are looking for a job. Everybody's why is different. Everybody is unique and in a different place in their life. We may have similar WHYs, but they are all unique to us.

For example, here was mine: My WHY was keeping my shelter (apartment/condo), no matter what. For me, a job meant making money. That was important to me because it meant earning the income necessary to keep my apartment, that I love so much, and made me feel independent. I did NOT want to go crawling back home to live with my parents--that just wasn't me. So my biggest concern was not losing the apartment I had worked my butt off to rent. Your why could be very different. But we need to know what it is, so you can stay focused on **WHY** you are doing this.

What will a job provide you? (Write it out in this space)

Okay, now that you know what it will provide, <u>why</u> is that important? What do you need it for?

Is that ultimately your 'WHY"? If not, drill down deeper, keep asking yourself "Why?" until you get to the core reason.

Once you get there, complete this:

My "WHY" is:

Never forget your **WHY**. This is your motivation. When you have a
crappy day and feel super low, come back and read this, so you
remember your **WHY**. Stay focused on your **WHY**. Let it drive you.
Let it inspire you. Let it motivate you to kick some butt each and
every day! We will come back to this shortly, so stay tuned!

Next, read Chapter 3...don't fret...it's short and sweet...but VERY
important!

"Get out of bed.
Work out.
Kick ass.
Repeat.
YOU GOT THIS!"
~Miss OMG

Chapter 3
GET YOUR BUTT OUT OF BED & GET GOING

If you are fortunate enough to have someone supporting you, even for temporary, then it helps. Some people are not so lucky, and if you are one of those people, your challenge is to find something, anything, to pay for your bare necessities immediately.

So what to do?

Many people advised that it would take me a long time to break into my career and that I may have to "settle" with some sort of "get me by job" for a bit. Sadly, they were kind of right that it would take awhile, and yes I took on a "get me by job to pay my bills." But I did not let that derail me from my goal!

Here's how you turn this around on Day 1 of your NEW CAREER ADVENTURE!

First, you need to start a new routine. Now truth be told, the routine you may want to start is to hole-up and do nothing because you don't know where to start. HOWEVER, reality is that every second you hole up hiding, it is a another second that someone else is getting to put themself forward for a new job that could have been yours! So get your booty outta bed and get going!

What I did while I was unemployed: (I will outline later again for **YOU**, so just take a moment to absorb this scenario first)

My Morning Routine:

1) I got out of bed no later than 7am every morning, and made the bed. (Reason this is important: already productive and a lot less tempting to get back in)
2) I immediately exercised a minimum of 30 minutes first thing (usually 60 minutes—and made up some different daily routines just to shake things up a little)
3) Reviewed My To Do List (Of course on Day 1 I started putting together the initial To Do List)
4) Briefly checked my truly important messages (email)
5) Knocked out my Top 3-5 priorities off my To Do List before lunch

My Afternoon Routine:

1) Lunch—20 minute healthy lunch plus a short 10 minute walk (I kinda liked the walking part, so for me, over time I found myself spending less time eating and more time walking when the weather was nice—and on occasion I would grab a sandwich and a water bottle and ate while I walked. Multi-tasking!)
2) Briefly checked my truly important messages (email), again
3) Lists Review
4) Networking
5) Job Searching

My Evening Routine: (This was super hard for me at first)

1) Discovered some hobbies, and engaged in them
2) TALKED (not just emailed/texted) to 1 or 2 friends/family members, made coffee dates, walk & talk dates, tennis dates, etc. to meet with friends in person and chat, to stay connected (and dream together)
3) Went to bed at a normal hour to get a good night's rest

Now I want you to know that I changed this up a lot from what I did when I was in college to being a "real grown-up" now. You are lucky. You have the latest and greatest program that I went through all the hard knocks of life to develop for you. You're welcome. So flashforward to when I was suddenly seeking a new career opportunity some years back---doesn't matter that I was old as dirt, (LOL!), the same routine is applicable for you, your friends seeking first or early careers or event if you have a parent (or know an older person) who loses their job, you encourage them to read this book and they could apply and customize to their own situation too.

The first day I put this in action, I went to my very best friend's house and we sat in her pool at the end of a long, but productive day. (Luckily, we were still experiencing California Indian Summer in October). I shared with her my woes about finding a job. She listened, shared some of her own experiences, and then we both began something very positive. We began to dream out loud together. She shared her dreams of writing a children's book, which encouraged me to I confide that I had always been encouraged to write books too. As a former journalist, I had always wished I had time to go back to writing again. We both encouraged each other—and you know what? Six months later, for better or worse, I published my first Miss OMG book. (The fact that I wrote a book in the humor genre, while I was dealing with such emotional distress at the time just baffles me at the irony! But "they" say laughter is the best medicine, right)? The point is, you need to take some time to dream out loud. Explore new ideas, even if they end up only being hobbies, because they can become very healthy outlets.

It is important to get YOUR daily routine together immediately and stay connected to people. Even though you may feel like you are in a job-finding-fog, just do this. Go through the motions of the routine everyday, NO MATTER WHAT. Soon it will become a comfort to you. Soon you will find excitement to look forward to each day. Soon you will discover that this horrible thing that happened to you has created a new life adventure, and you are on an expedition to find your next or first job, your next or first career, or maybe a business venture—whatever the case may be for you—and if you begin to learn some new things about yourself, well that is just icing on the cake!

> ### Vela
>
> When Vela lost her job, she found herself dealing with more than job loss, she found herself trying to cope with overwhelming sadness. So much so, that she spent most of her time hiding out in her bedroom. She shared, "I did not look for a job for 6 months. I just maxed out my credit card and lived off of my parents."
>
> Without support of a career coach or a guide to help her get going again as she waded through her sadness, it took Vela over two months to get a grip on trying to find a new job, and over six months to attain one.
>
> Morale of the story: Stay in motion and gather support. You can do this!

LESSON: DAY 1-GET YOUR BUTT OUT OF BED & GET GOING

"Get out of bed.
Work out.
Kick ass.
Repeat.
YOU GOT THIS!"
~Miss OMG

USE PENCIL FOR THIS EXERCISE!
After you've read Chapter 3: **GET YOUR BUTT OUT OF BED & GET GOING,** respond to the following:

Ultimately, what is your goal in this new career adventure?

Now let's get specific. So, specifically speaking, what does that mean?

How will you know that you've accomplished this? In other words, how are you going to measure the success of reaching that goal?

Is that attainable? If not, then go back and change--it's okay! You may change this a few times...no worries.

Now that you have an attainable goal, stop and ask yourself, is it really realistic? Could you realistically attain that goal based on the criteria you have set? If not, tweak until you truly have a reasonable and realistic goal for this job search adventure.

Ok, last, set a time on it. How long are you REASONABLY giving yourself to attain this goal?

Now write out the whole thing:
My goal is to (include the timeframe):

I will know that I have reached it by:

Fantastic! Now you have a SMART goal set for yourself, which means you are setting yourself up for success. WAY TO GO!

Now open up the inside of your spiral notebook/binder. Copy your **WHY** on the inside cover, and then copy your **GOAL**. This will serve as an additional visual for you. If and when you ever doubt yourself, or you are having an off day, open up you notebook and read to yourself. Sometimes we just need a little reminding. (If you are using a 3-ring binder, slip this into a clear window view in the front of your binder so you see it all the time)! I also recommend that you write it on the inside cover of this guidebook...so you always have it handy!

Ok, you've got most of your pre-planning done so you can hit the ground running. Now we move on to the nitty gritty.

Day 1: HOW TO GET STARTED WHEN I CAN BARELY START MYSELF? This chapter discusses establishing <u>YOUR</u> daily routine.

It is important to get YOUR daily routine together immediately and stay connected to people. Go through the motions of the routine everyday, NO MATTER WHAT.

So go read Chapter 4, then get your supplies together, and get ready to start working on reaching your goals.
This IS happening! You are getting ready to tackle Day 1. (Now keep in mind, the expectation is that you are reading this the evening before you implement Day 1, to prepare yourself...but if you have the day set aside, and want to get started now, go for it)! Let's do this!!!

"I've got so many mountains to climb and goals to conquer.
I've got so many scars I want to leave on the planet.
I just feel like I'm not there yet.
I feel like I am just getting started."
~Nikki Sixx

Chapter 4
DAY 1: HOW TO GET STARTED WHEN I CAN BARELY START MYSELF?

You're probably dazed, confused and pretty much not knowing which way is up when you are first trying to figure out how to find a job, let alone a career. Not to worry, that is what this book is for! Following these steps will help you put the wheels in motion, even when you may not know which way you are headed. So get ready, because this is a full day!

A few things to help you be prepared for the day—first, figure out a system of timers. I use my phone and good ole Google, but others prefer setting a kitchen timer on their desk, while some use their favorite electronic device (artificial intelligence) to remind them. I prefer some sort of AI/phone app so I can set it and forget it and not constantly feel like I need to look at the timer itself—cuz it just wastes, well, er...you know...TIME!

Today will be different than the rest of the week, because today we are working on various components of looking for a job. We are gathering the "parts" for success. (For those of you who are new to this job finding business, it may be a lot of new stuff to take in. Hang in there, and trust the process). All these parts we work on today are critical, and will help you to make lots of headway everyday from here on out.

Be prepared to feel overwhelmed. <u>You should feel that way</u>. I am going to throw a lot at you today. This will be the hardest day, then it all gets easier and easier after today. Here's the deal, we are NOT going to tip-toe into this new job of looking for a job. Tip-toeing is for wimps. You are not a wimp. Right? Right!

You need to be a go-getter, and go-getters go full force with gusto into whatever it is that they are going and getting. So get in that mindset now. You ARE a go-getter, BE a go-getter! Now let's go-get!

You should be so flippin' busy today that you do NOT notice the time and think to yourself, "What? It's ONLY 10am?" Instead, you should be thinking, "OH WOW, it's <u>already</u> 10am, where is the time going?" That's your cue that you are getting into the zone, and that's where you need to be to get back on track!

Get it? Got it? Good.

Now go get your (doctor-approved) exercise in and eat breakfast, because there is no time to break until lunch. Here we go:

Day 1-

1) Get an old-fashioned spiral notebook and keep with you at all times (you will use this guidebook you are reading as your resource notebook)...thoughts and ideas are going to hit you at the weirdest times and you need to write them down the second they strike. For today, if you don't have these, use scratch paper until you get to the store or can bum a notbook off someone. (NO EXCUSES)! You can also use a binder with divided sections of binder paper...but you will still need at least a small notebook to keep with you at all times, in case inspiration strikes! (If nothing else, slip a pad of sticky notes into your purse, or several sticky notes into your wallet—just be sure to swap them out when you add those notes to your "real" notebook, as a back-up plan. Don't have sticky notes? Still no excuse—get a piece of copy paper or two and fold them up and slip them into your wallet/purse).

Also, there is a reason we are NOT doing this technique on a computer—I know it is strange in this day and age, but just trust the process. Studies have proven we are more apt to reach our goals and be more successful if we hand write. (So using old school notebooks are the best method for what we are trying to accomplish).

2) Put together your schedule for the day—WRITE IT OUT! This means skimming through the tasks I have below for you and write them out. I recommend aiming for completing #3-5 before lunch, to the best of your ability, and working on the components for #6 after lunch (I have helped you for the first week-- you will see a condensed version after the narrative version, but next week, you are on you own for writing it out)!

3) Put your Resume on Notice
If you've never put together a resume, you need to, NOW! If you already have one, get it out and be sure it is all updated. (You will need it IMMEDIATELY for your LinkedIN profile, Indeed and other job search platforms).

Please keep in mind that you need a General Resume and then what I call a "Template Resume" (one that can be customized for special job applications, as needed)

For your resume, you need to list your skill-sets first, remember employers may get hundreds of resumes for one post, so it is important that your resume passes a paper screening.

(AUTHOR'S NOTE: Just a tip that you will want to get your resume into the hands of friends and colleagues who can deliver it to the hiring managers, VPs, Presidents, etc of companies. This extra effort can make a big difference in getting your resume seen. So make it a priority to get your resume done this week)! Also, this is a KEY way that your family and friends who mean well, can actually help you with their leads! YOU are the one who needs to do the work to get the job, but if they can get your resume into the hands of someone who will review it, WHAHOO, that helps)!

4) Sign-up for Unemployment
Regardless of whether you think you can collect it or not, that is if you have held a paying job before (with a real paycheck and taxes withheld and all that stuff), just in case. The worst they can do is decline your application.

5) Update your Social Media
If you are not on Social Media, today is the day to embrace it. It can be your best friend during events like this: At bare minimum you need LinkedIn and Facebook.

Keep in mind—**do not go on a rant about how you lost your job on your Social Media, or how a company refused to hire you, etc.**—this will turn people off and they will tune you out. There is a difference between posting your hatred of a company who you feel did you wrong and simply putting out there, "Friends-I am looking for leads in the blah, blah, blah industry. Please private message me if you hear of anything." People want to help when you are being positive. So, increase your positive frequency, (regardless of how hippy dippy that may sound), and put out good vibes. People like good vibes. They also like funny and happy—even if you aren't feeling so funny and happy at the moment. Search for motivational memes if needed and share them out on your pages. Share positive stories—be a positive ray of sunshine for those to notice. (Plus all that positivity may keep you from burning bridges)!

Clean up your social media and delete anything that you have posted that may not present you in the best light to a prospective employer—because yes, they search you out on your social media. So even if it is legal where you live, delete the hysterical photo of you and your buds smokin' buds. Delete those photos of you doing keg stands. Delete any harsh posts that you may have been spewing in some sort of rage. It is imperative.

Be sure to be a ray of professional sunshine. Do include your posts from your participation in community work or charitable events, etc. Ask friends (behind the scenes) to post public comments of gratitude for how you went above and beyond to help in some sort of generous situation (as long as it is truthful). In other words, paint yourself on social media, in the light of being a stellar human being...and delete anything that could cause questioning by of potential employer.

6) Make lists:
   In this guidebook, you will have some lists to fill out. If you need to add even more, feel free to tear out and add to a notebook/binder. This is guidebook will serve as a resource notebook of sorts for you, and as alluded to, we

are going to work on lists right now.

First-**NETWORKING/CONTACTS LIST**. Make a list of everybody you know who you might have a possible lead, could keep you in mind for a job, or who would promote the heck out of you if they run into someone seeking a person of your talents. The longer the list the better. Yes, think about all those older people you have known your whole life, etc. too! (We will go over this a little later when we discuss The Daily 3, so stay tuned). Keep adding daily as you think of people or hear about people you should contact. Think especially about people you know who are networking gurus, super connected, those people who seem to know everybody.

Second-**REFERENCES LIST**. Make a list of 5-10 people you can immediately ask to write you Letters of Recommendation/Reference.

Third-**BUSINESS LIST**. Start making a list of businesses, companies, organizations, (places of employment) all around you or where ever you'd be willing to relocate (if necessary). Continuously add to this list—daily if possible!

Fourth-**JOB SEARCH ENGINE LIST**. Make a list of employment search programs: Indeed, ZipRecruiter, GlassDoor, Linked In, EdJoin.org, Temp. Agencies, etc., and register an account for each, if you don't have one already. While LinkedIn presents itself as a social media site, it is actually a great place to go when looking for jobs.

Fifth-**"I TOTALLY ROCK" LIST**. Begin making a two column list:
(Left Side) Your Strengths (What are you good at? It can be anything. Master at Excel, Google Maniac, Marketing Guru, Project Manager Extraordinaire.

Whatever you rock at. Stuck on this? Think personal first then: Maybe you are the best peanut butter and jelly sandwich maker in the world—list it, and go from there, if you need to!)
(Right Side) What do you like to do? (Hobbies, pastimes, have-always-wanted-to-do/learn things)

7) Now, open a fresh page in your spiral notebook (or binder). This is going to become your **DAILY JOURNAL**. Trust me it's not the froo-froo kind of journal you are thinking of, and it really works. So stay with me, don't check out, this is going to be great—REALLY!

First, make two columns, from top to about the last 2-3 inches of the page.(I just simply draw a line down the center of the page, then a perpendicular line across. It does not have to be perfect, so put your ruler/straightedge away).

1/23 TO DO LIST	TODAY'S ACCOMPLISHMENTS

NOTES:

For the first column you need to list **TO DO LIST**:

Today's won't be as full, but as you think of stuff, write it down.

For the second column, list **TODAY'S ACCOMPLISHMENTS**

So let's take a moment right now and do that.

Go back through #1-6 above and bullet key things you were able to do today. Even if it was simply stuff like: "Started Resume Revision," "Began List of Networking Contacts," "Set up Facebook account." That's okay, because it is all progress! You need to see what you were able to get done.

At the bottom of the page, you have written "**NOTES**." This is for important things that have come up during the day that you want to "document" or maybe just not forget. (This sort of Daily Journal is a great practice to get into, even after you find your next job. Because you will be in the practice of writing down your accomplishments, you'll easily be able to share with your future employer the positive contributions you've been making for the company, etc. So keep on writing—besides, the mind can only remember so much. Give your brain a break!)

Now turn the page, and write tomorrow's date, and replicate the template. Now we are going to work on tomorrow's **TO DO LIST,** today:

Go back through #1-6 above again, and this time list everything you still need to accomplish. If it isn't complete, it goes on the list. Now keep in mind, some of the things

> you've done today are an ongoing process. So if you haven't started a "list" it needs to be on the To Do List. If you have started a list, you'll find it may become part of your daily routine for awhile. You will need to set aside time to review your lists daily (and always add to them the moment you think of someone/something who/that needs to be added).

This is a busy day, but you can do it—and you kinda have the time now to do it, right? So get going! Jumping right in and being proactive will make a difference—with finding a job faster and with working through the eratic feelings you may be dealing with. For now, finding a job IS your job. Welcome to working for YOU!

JD

JD was skeptical when he started on Day 1 with "The Lists." He shares, "On the first day I felt like I needed some direction to get started, because I needed a good plan on what to do to get going. But I was also hesitant on what this all (the lists) was about. Once I started using it, and writing out my accomplishments it started showing me the positives and gave me the frame of mind that, yes, I am making progress and getting things completed. It gives the positive self-feedback that I am doing things."

So, it is VERY important, because there are times when you may feel like you haven't accomplished anything, if you don't use this part of the system. He adds, "Some days are better than others, because personal stuff sometimes comes up, so maybe you don't get as much done with the job search, but you're still accomplishing things." It kind of shows you a balance of personal life with job search life.

When it came to the "Daily 3," JD was extremely resistant. His personality type is absolutely adverse to asking for help, and allowing the assistance of a career coach was a huge step itself, let alone being asked to take it a step further and reach out &

---

network.

JD explains, "At first I didn't want to do it. I needed to be coached and encouraged to do this. I don't like reaching out, it's not my personality to reach out and ask for help. But with persistent coaching and guidance, I tried it and found it to be helpful." He shares he discovered some important aspects to this technique, "(Networking) led to people giving suggestions, leads, other contacts, and actual support & a willingness to help in anyway they can. It is still hard for me because it pushes my comfort zone." But by doing this he has even experienced some renewed professional relationships. Which is very valuable in both work and personal life.

LESSON: Day 1-To Do List
Now let's put all of this reading together. First, be sure you set up your Daily Journal as the reading suggested. Open up the notebook you have designated as your "Daily Journal." Set up the first page as such:

1/23 TO DO LIST	TODAY'S ACCOMPLISHMENTS

NOTES:

Now add these tasks to your **To Do List** for TODAY:

- Setup your Daily Journal Binder
- Write out your schedule
- Resume Review
- Sign up for Unemployment
- Update your Social Media
- Make your lists in second notebook

For each thing you accomplish, cross it off and add it to the TODAY'S ACCOMPLISHMENTS side of the page. While this may seem redundant, there is a reason for this. You are getting into the habit of writing down your accomplishments.
(You will repeat this structure for each page in your Daily Journal).

Next Step, let's set up your schedule for **DAY 1**. It is different than the rest of the week, but stick to it as close as you can. (This routine will evolve over the next couple of days. By Day 4 you will have your solid routine put together). Keep in mind that you are using the details from the guidebook to guide you through the following tasks.

DAY 1 Schedule:

7:00am-	**30 minutes Doctor-approved exercise**
7:30am-	**Breakfast/shower, etc.**
8:00am-	**Getting organized**
9:00am-	**Resume Review & Exercise Lesson**
10:00am-	**Sign up for Unemployment** (you may or may not be eligible, but hey, it's worth a try, right?)
11:00am-	**Update your Social Media & Exercise Lesson**
Noon-	**Break for lunch** (Try to go for a short walk if possible, or get some sort of movement in)
1:00pm	**Create Networking/Contacts List (provided for you)**
1:30pm	**Create Reference List (provided for you)**
2:00pm	**Create Business List** (Places of potential employment) **(provided for you)**
2:30pm	**Create Job Search Engine List (provided for you)**

3:00pm	**Create "I Totally Rock" List** (provided for you)
3:30pm	**Update today's Accomplishments List**
3:45pm	**Set for Success** (Set-up tomorrow's To Do List/Accomplishments Page)
4:00pm	**Read Day 2: Seize the Day**; then take the rest of the day off and **decompress!!!**

DAY 1 EXERCISES (I know you are reading ahead, but for these exercises, do <u>during your ACTUAL Day 1</u>)

Resume Review:

Take out your resume.

When was the last time it was updated? You might not even have one! No worries.

If you have one, review your resume for accuracy and mark it up. Don't be shy, this is your time to discover what makes you shine.

Circle key titles and tasks. As you think of others, scribble them on the resume.

IF YOU DO OR DON'T HAVE ONE: You need to take some time to also review current resumes styles. Nowadays, key roles & skill sets tend to be listed first, rather than a timeline of jobs/positions held, because you need to pass a paper screening. (Save that for later). Go to the internet and type in **21st Century Resume Templates**. Review and see which ones speak to you. Over the next few days you will build/update your resume in this fashion.

UPDATE YOUR SOCIAL MEDIA:

1) Take some time to go through your social media platform(s). Review your posts.
2) Do you have any negative posts? Any rants? Anything unsavory or inappropriate in the eyes of a potential employer? TAKE IT DOWN.
3) Next, do you have any photos from positive events (think helping your community, charitable events, etc.)? Be sure to "casually" edit posts to let people know which charity you are helping out, etc. Use your Social Media to put your best foot forward and to shine.
4) Add some positivity images and motivational memes. Not your thing? Make it your thing, **for now**. Potential employers will scour our social media and they want to hire people who are positive and do positive things.

CREATE YOUR LISTS:

On the pages to follow are the lists you need to make. Remember, this guidebook is serving as a resource notebook for you, however, you are welcome to pull these pages out and add to a 3 ring binder if that works better for you. Do what feels right for you)!

Here we go! These will be "moving parts" today, but tomorrow, you will put them all together. Think of it as a jigsaw puzzle today, you are just getting the pieces ut and ready to go, and tomorrow you put the puzzle together.

NETWORKING/CONTACTS LIST

Make a list of everybody you know who you might have a possible lead, could keep you in mind for a job, or who would promote the heck out of you if they run into someone seeking a person of your talents. The longer the list the better. (We will go over this a little later, so stay tuned). Keep adding daily as you think of people or hear about people you should contact. Think especially about people you know who are networking gurus, super connected, those people who seem to know everybody & add an * next to them.

1. _____	21. _____
2. _____	22. _____
3. _____	23. _____
4. _____	24. _____
5. _____	25. _____
6. _____	26. _____
7. _____	27. _____
8. _____	28. _____
9. _____	29. _____
10. _____	30. _____
11. _____	31. _____
12. _____	32. _____
13. _____	33. _____
14. _____	34. _____
15. _____	35. _____
16. _____	36. _____
17. _____	37. _____
18. _____	38. _____
19. _____	39. _____
20. _____	40. _____

REFERENCES LIST

Make a list of 5-10 people you can immediately ask to write you Letters of Recommendation/Reference

1. _____

2. _____

3. _____

4. _____

5. _____

6. _____

7. _____

8. _____

9. _____

10. _____

BUSINESS LIST-Start making a list of businesses (places of employment) all around you or where ever you'd be willing to relocate (if necessary). Continuously add to this list!

1. _____	21. _____
2. _____	22. _____
3. _____	23. _____
4. _____	24. _____
5. _____	25. _____
6. _____	26. _____
7. _____	27. _____
8. _____	28. _____
9. _____	29. _____
10. _____	30. _____
11. _____	31. _____
12. _____	32. _____
13. _____	33. _____
14. _____	34. _____
15. _____	35. _____
16. _____	36. _____
17. _____	37. _____
18. _____	38. _____
19. _____	39. _____
20. _____	40. _____

JOB SEARCH ENGINE LIST

Make a list of employment search programs and register an account for each, (if you don't have one already).

1. _____

2. _____

3. _____

4. _____

5. _____

6. _____

7. _____

8. _____

9. _____

10. _____

"I TOTALLY ROCK" LIST

LIST YOUR STRENGTHS: What are you great at? What can NO ONE take away from you?	HOBBIES/PASTIMES/STUFF YOU'VE ALWAYS WANTED TO DO:
1. _____	1. _____
2. _____	2. _____
3. _____	3. _____
4. _____	4. _____
5. _____	5. _____
6. _____	6. _____
7. _____	7. _____
8. _____	8. _____
9. _____	9. _____
10. _____	10. _____
11. _____	11. _____
12. _____	12. _____
13. _____	13. _____
14. _____	14. _____
15. _____	15. _____
16. _____	16. _____
17. _____	17. _____
18. _____	18. _____
19. _____	19. _____
20. _____	20. _____

DAY 2 PREP:

YAY! You did it! You got through Day 1. Now take some time to set yourself up for success by reading about Chapter 5 of the Finding It Guidebook. Keep in mind that the chapters in the guidebook are super short and will provide you the background information on this program and what's to come for the day you are tackling, so that you may begin to understand whys and the how of using this program. As always, trust the process!

"You can't spell 'challenge' without 'change.'
If you're going to rise to the challenge,
you have to be prepared to change."
~Author Unknown

Chapter 5
DAY 2: SEIZE THE DAY!!!
(AKA: Putting all the parts and pieces together day)

Yesterday was hard. I remember my Day 1, and seriously, my brain felt tired by the end of the day. I was dealing with my feelings of anxiety about looking for a job, (instead of planning out my Summer Break of adventures), which was what I was used to doing. What a dose of reality! Plus, looking for a job in my industry living in a Top Market area, was next to impossible. Regardless, I made a lot of headway that first day. And again, it was hard—so I get it.

I'm not going to tell you that future days won't be as hard, because reality is that life can truly be a kick in the groin. But you are not going to lay on the ground wallowing in pain and self-pity cursing 'til the cows come home. You are going to pull yourself up, dust yourself off and get your butt in gear, again. (And again, and again, and again). Because you are on an adventure here! So let's get ready to tackle Day 2 of this job finding expedition.

By now you should have your schedule for today and bazillions of lists already started that I assigned you yesterday. You have set yourself up for success with all the organization you did yesterday. My guess is that you've gotten up at a reasonable time, made the bed, exercised and had some sort of resemblance of a breakfast. Right? Right. (And if you are saying "WRONG" right now, stop, drop and get it together, because you are worth it! You are worth making the effort to have a successful day. You are worthy of the progress you are going to make today. So right your wrongs if you need to, and let's get going—there's no time to waste)!

Now let's do Day 2: Putting it all together

7:00am 30 min. Doctor-Approved exercise
7:30am Breakfast/shower, etc.
8:00am Check your email/texts
- Get in the habit of only checking it 2-3 times per day
- Check at 8am, 1pm and maybe 5pm—spend no more than 30 minutes and set a timer if need be.
- Scan it first for any "important" emails/texts, and respond to those first. If you have time left over in your 30 minute allotment, then respond to other less priority emails, but when time is up, it is up. (Here's the deal, some people may be finding out that you are job hunting or they just aren't motivated to do so and might want to enable you to blow it off, and they may be sending you tons of texts/emails. The words of encouragement are awesome, and yes you need to respond, but it can be a downer and time suck to spend all day doing this. (And the invites are nice, but we all know that blowing this off is a quick trip to getting nowhere on your goals). A quick way to wade through this is to send out the following response to every message:

  "Hey, thanks for touching base with me. I am busy today seeking out career opportunities and am super excited about it. Would really like to chat with you soon and maybe pique your brain for leads, etc. If you have any, please email them to me. I promise I will get back to you sooner than later. Thanks much,

---

talk soon."

Obviously you are going to word it the way you need in order to sound like you.

But you need to stay focused, so this message serves a bunch of purposes:

- It helps friends and family to know you are alive and responsive & in the midst of being a go-getter!
- It kindly lets them know you need a to focus on you and your career search right now.
- It lets them know you are looking for leads—and it lets them know they can help you by sending you leads
- And, it buys you a little time so that you can get into your new routine of your new Looking for a Job job, so you aren't derailed from your newfound focus

If you end up with extra time today, great! Call them and chat, but not during your "work hours."

A couple tips, if this is a struggle for you:
- Mute the chimes on your email/text notifications
- Log-off your email/turn off your phone all together---YUP, hardcore move, but it's bold and brash and can help you kick some ass!

8:30am GET FOCUSED & STAY FOCUSED
Get your notebooks—the one for all your LISTS & NOTES (This guidebook), and your DAILY JOURNAL one too (the spiral or binder).
■ First glance over yesterday's journal entry. Take a look at what you accomplished and be proud. Then take a look at Today's To Do List.
■ You need to prioritize the To Do List and get

at least the top three most important things on that list done before lunch today.

- Also, as you accomplish things today, please enter them on today's journal page under, (yep, you guessed it), "Today's Accomplishments."

PLEASE NOTE: At times you will have some personal stuff to add to your TO DO LIST. That's okay. But remember to approach this system as a job, and you would not normally be taking care of a bunch of personal things during your "work day," right? If you find that you are, a simple solution is to get up an extra hour earlier everyday and carve out "Personal To Do List Time" during your morning. Another idea is to add that extra hour to your lunchtime to complete personal tasks, or at the end of the day. This way you remain dedicated and focused on your job of job hunting.

Knock out 3-5 of your top priorities on your To Do List (Try to pick the crappiest thing on your To Do List to do first, get it done and then everything else will feel like a cakewalk). NO PROCRASTINATING! Just jump in and get it done! You will feel great as you cross it off and add it to your Accomplishments List for the day.

12:30pm LUNCHTIME-Take 30 and try to decompress (walk or get some sort of movement for 10+ minutes) You really need to stop and take a break. Make yourself. I know it can be easy to get in your zone with all of this and not want to stop, but your brain needs a break—and your body needs nourishment. So stop n' slurp some soup or somethin'!

1:00pm 30 MINUTE EMAIL CHECK
- Stick with the routine: Scan for important emails, then with time left over, respond to those who are checking in
- Thank those who send you leads, and add your

leads to your to your lists.

1:30pm LISTS REVIEW TIME (This will become faster as time goes on)

- First review the **NETWORKING/CONTACTS LIST** you've been working on, add anymore that come to mind.

- TODAY'S TASKS
  - Search your email address book and add those you've forgotten, if any.

  - Add people from your Facebook, LinkedIn & other social media circles who might be helpful.

  - Think of individuals from your last workplace (if you have one) who you might be able to reach out to.

    IMPORTANT: this becomes part of your daily routine, so do it diligently, add it to your accomplishments, and move on to:

- SELECT YOUR DAILY 3

  Your DAILY 3 are the three people you need to contact the most, in order to reach out and professionally holler for help! Start by picking your heavy-hitter, super-connected people. THIS SHOULD BE THREE NEW PEOPLE EVERYDAY. Your message to them should be brief and simple, but also personal. Something like:

  > *"Hey Susan,*
  > *Hope you are doing well.*
  > *How's (blah, blah, blah—insert something sincere and personal here) going?*

I was wondering if you are aware of any opportunities that may be coming available with (such & such company), that might utilize my skills and talents with (insert what you basically do—ie: Public Relations and Strategic Social Media Marketing)? I am exploring new employment opportunities and would be grateful if you would keep me in mind if you know or hear of anything.

Thanks so much, would enjoy chatting with you when you have some time!

~Michele"

(Be sure to add each person you sent this to, to your Today's Accomplishments, and to your To Do List for a week from today, in order to schedule a Follow-up).

- Next for TODAY, you need to email those 5-10 people you listed on your **REFERENCES LIST** and ask them if they will be references for you, and if they would kindly write you Letters of Recommendation. These letters are very important to some companies/industries. Much like the Daily 3 message, make it brief, but also make it sincere and personal. You can do this quickly by re-using the basics of the same letter, but be sure to personalize it each time! Give yourself 1 hour to get this done...set the timer and GO! (Then add each person you sent to on your Today's Accomplishments list)! YAY!

- Now let's put that **BUSINESSES LIST** to work for the next 60-90 minutes

    Today seek out each company's CAREERS/JOBS section on their website, and BOOKMARK it! If you need to register a profile, do it.

    Next peruse it and see what they've got. This takes more time in the beginning, but gets faster as you review daily for any updates

    Repeat for each company until your time is up for the day—be sure to add the companies you searched to your Today's Accomplishments List, and the others you will get tomorrow (or if you have a little spare time later today).

- It's time for more Job Searching via the job search engine applications. For the next 60-90 minutes spend your time exploring jobs from your **JOB SEARCH ENGINE LIST**. If you come across new sites, add them to your list so that they become part of your new daily routine.

    Be sure to upload your resume. If it isn't done, try to throw together a slam dunk one for the moment, and then update your resumes in these search engines once you have the final complete. (Keep in mind, these applications usually use a general resume, but occasionally you may need to customize it for various job applications, depending on the site). For example, my resume for Indeed is a broad resume of all my skill-sets, whereas my EdJoin.org resume is customized to highlight my attributes in the education world.

Be aware that sometimes the search engines that automatically send you leads, may send you stuff you are not interested in at all. Who knows why? Over-sensitive to Keywords, maybe? But review and quickly move on. (You may find some repetition as well, again, review and move on. Also re-check your parameters on a regular basis).

- **I TOTALLY ROCK LIST**

  You are probably wondering why I include this? Well it is simple, these are areas that you may want to add to your resume and your cover letters. Employers want to know that they are getting a quality person with great skills and talents, (and sometimes we need to remind ourselves what in the world those are, especially during wen job hunting). Remember to add attributes that no one could ever take away from you, not even a crappy employer.

  So for someone like me, no one can take away my excellent skills in communicating, organizational strategies & sustainable systems development, high energy, and natural leadership & management by positive motivation abilities. Because at the end of the day, when you strip it all down, that's me. That's who I am.

  So who ARE you? What can no one ever take away from you?

  Make sure to glance at this list on a regular basis—(I actually like to glance at it first thing in the morning and last thing for the work day…because it reminds me that I am Michele "Frickin'-Awesome-Super-Successful-at-whatever-she-does"

Giacomini, and I'm on an adventure to see who it going to be lucky enough to add me to their team)! So there. (Yes, it does feel good to say that—rather empowering, actually—I encourage you to try it)!

There is another reason we use the I TOTALLY ROCK LIST, but it comes up in a couple of days and I don't want to ruin the surprise, so hang tight!

5:00pm- Get ready to call it a day.
First, be sure you've written down all your Accomplishments
Second, transfer any TO DOs over to tomorrow's List
If you have any left over time before 5pm, do some more networking:

Respond to people who have reached out to you, or reach out to 1 or 2 more people on your Contacts List.
Third, read the guidebook's **DAY 3: OH MY GAWD, HOW WILL I PAY MY BILLS?**
Fourth, when it is 5pm today, your work day is over. So it is time to play. Look at your **HOBBIES/INTERESTS LISTS.** Is there something on it you can do this evening? Anything you can schedule for later this week or the following weekend? Want to learn to paint? Draw? Something else? Look up YouTube Videos for tutorials. Dust off that book you've been meaning to read. Shoot hoops. Go for a long walk and think about all the positive things you've accomplished today. Be proud. You've got this! (And seriously take the night off—if you suddenly think of something, jot it down in your notebook real quick for tomorrow...in the

meantime, go chill out. For a bonus, write down some gratitude or a "bright side" of the day in your notes section.

In all, staying positive and looking at your next career or job opportunity as a new and exciting adventure will help to keep up your morale, and keep your eye on the prize of finding your next job. It's all about positive attitude!

Bryan

In 2017, Bryan took a "gap semester" to decide what he wanted to do, and spend more time with his family.

College just wasn't working for him. After four years of starting classes and never feeling motivated to complete most of them because he just couldn't see the point, he knew he needed to take some time and figure out what he wanted to do with his life.

So Bryan decided to meet up with his brother Derek and travel through Asia and Australia together for a couple of months or so.

During this time away from friends and most of his family, Bryan gave himself permission to think about what HE wanted to do with his life. Did he really want to finish college? Did he want to go to tech school? What were his interests? What were his talents? What were his passions? What could he see himself making money at and enjoying?

For Bryan, it all kept coming back to real estate.

When he returned home after his self-reflection journey, he immediately enrolled in real estate classes and completed them right away. He took the test to become an agent and passed it the first time. How did that happen? What the dramatic change? Why so suddenly successful? Because he is smart and he was interested in what he was learning about, so it made a HUGE difference in how he attacked his "education."

He secured his first career job fairly quickly using the Finding It program (on an abbreviated schedule-found later in this book), and this lead him to an incredible career as a Property Manager and Leasing Agent for a large company with much room for

---

growth, very good pay, and benefits!

As a result of his proactive mentality, Bryan is already seeing the rewards of success!

(See, I told you it was short)! And just as short is today's lesson...not a bunch of exercises today. Just some roll-up your sleeves and get going on your new daily routine stuff! Feel free to use this area to make notes, cross out, add to, etc on your schedule and get moving)!

LESSON: DAY 2-SEIZE THE DAY!!!

Yesterday all your hard work & organization set yourself up for success.

Today we begin to put all these pieces together.

1) Glance over yesterday's journal entry and be proud of your accomplishments
2) Re-familiarize yourself with Today's To Do List
3) Note that today's schedule is a bit different--stick with it!
4) Refer to the guidebook for the details for each task below

DAY 2 SCHEDULE:
7:00 am/or earlier- 30+ minutes doctor-approved exercise
7:30 am-   Breakfast/Shower, etc
8:00 am-   Check your email (set your timer for 30 min.)
8:30 am-12:30 pm- Priority TO DO LIST Tasks--Stay

focused!

NOTE: The guidebook has some priority tasks for you to do today, be sure you add those to your list and get them done!

12:30 pm-	**Lunchtime (Try to get in some sort of 10+ min movement)**
1:00 pm-	**Check your email (set your timer for 30 min.)**
1:30 pm-	**LISTS Review Time**

Start with Networking/Contacts List and make any additions you thought of overnight.
VERY IMPORTANT:
Select your Daily 3 and send a message or call.

References List-Email those 5-10 people and ask for letters of reference

Businesses List-For 60-90 min., seek out the CAREERS tabs on each of your businesses listed, for potential Opportunities. (Remember to bookmark)

Job Search Engine List-For 60-90 min. Seek out job opportunities on various job search engines. Set up profiles and automatic setting for these search engines to forward jobs of potential interest to you (if applicable).

I Totally Rock List-Review your Strengths and add any more that come to mind.

5:00pm-   **Get ready to call it a day.**

First, be sure you've written down all your Accomplishments
Second, transfer any TO DOs over to tomorrow's List
Third, read in the guidebook
DAY 3: OH MY GAWD, HOW WILL I PAY MY BILLS?
Fourth, check out your Hobbies/Interests List and go engage in something fun/interesting/relaxing. Whatever floats your boat!
Enjoy the rest of the night!

DAY 3 PREP:

Day 2 was different than Day 1, for sure. Did you see how all those parts you were gathering were starting to come together? It will become evident and the process will become quicker over the days to come. YOU'VE GOT THIS! Now let's get ready for Day 3. No extra exercises than the tasks prescribed in Day 3, so let's review and get going!

"I make myself rich,
by making my wants few."
~Henry David Thoreau

Chapter 6
DAY 3: OH MY GAWD, HOW WILL I PAY MY BILLS?

Today we need to add a few more things to your To Do List. If you haven't already, you may be starting to freak out about paying your bills. Hopefully, you are in a position that you will be okay and can scrape by for now, or even better. But some of us aren't so lucky. (Flashing forward many years, when my husband was laid off from his job of almost 18 years we lost close to 66% of our monthly income. OUCH! Much different from my 20s when I could have moved in with friends/family to save money for a bit)!

Well, you know how "they" say money doesn't buy everything? Well "they" do NOT know what "they" are talking about. Because money pays to keep a roof over our heads, money pays to keep clothing on our backs, and money sure as hell puts food on the table. So that said, there is a lot to be said about money...even if you are minimalistic.

The first thing we had to do was Trim the Fat. Quite frankly, compared to many, we were already living fairly lean. But we did it. It was not easy and definitely was painful, but at the same time, we were keeping our roof over our heads.

Could we have kept a "fatter" lifestyle? Sure! But it would have meant selling our forever home that we had found slightly over a year before.

Could we have given that up and moved in with friends or relatives? Sure. But it was not our goal.

Everybody has their own priorities. You need to figure out what yours are. Your roof may not be your top priority, as long as you have one somehow, someway—and that's okay.

What you need to remember what your "WHY" is. Your motivation for finding new employment. (If you are using this guidebook step-by-step, you already know what this is).

Maybe yours is your mode of transportation, or maybe you are an ultimate minimalist and have zero attachments—that's okay too! (And for you minimalists, I'd really like to grow up and be like you some day—but chances are it will never happen).

So we determined our priorities and set out to carve out chunks of change every which way we could. And if you are like we were and don't have some secret fortune stashed away somewhere, or have a massive trust you can just live off of, then you too may need to trim some fat—and I've got tips for you today as you work through your To Do List.

Speaking of which, please add these tasks to your To Do List for today:

- Trim the Fat
- Search Special Groups on Facebook
- Meet-ups
- Seek friends who recently switched careers/got laid off, etc.
- Find an Accountability Partner

So here's your schedule for today, please take some time to tweak it to fit for you. (By-the-way, there is a method to the madness of providing you these daily schedules. Wanna know the rationale? It is simple, I am helping you train yourself to structure your day. You do not have time to squander a day spinning on one thing, or even worse—doing nothing. Having a structured day is a great coping method as well. It sets you up for success, you accomplish more and at the end of the "work day" you feel good about being productive. So the sooner you get used to setting up a daily routine and schedule out your priorities, the faster you'll be on the road to success. Oh, and remember make your bed and exercise first thing)!

Let's do DAY 3-

7:00 am/or earlier-	**30+ minutes doctor-approved exercise**
7:30 am-	**Breakfast/Shower, etc**
8:00 am-	**Check your email (set your timer for 30 min.)**
8:30 am-	**DAILY AGENDA REVIEW/PRIORITY TASK TIME** (To Do List) Review yesterday's Accomplishments & Today's To Do List. Prioritize the To Do List and get at least the top three most important things on that list done before lunch today Remember to note Today's Accomplishments as you check off your To Do List
8:45 am-	**TRIM THE FAT** Saving money is making money right now. Go through your checking account, look at your auto pays, check your credit cards. (After today, make this a weekly thing—Fridays can be an especially good day, before the weekend comes to entice us to spend—it's like a little reality check before we go blowing a bunch of moola on

---

a weekend of fun). The objective is to pare down to the essentials, so that you don't have debt, or you have very little. Here are some ideas to get you started:

- Look for expenditures you really can cut back on. Do you need a wine of the month membership right now? Weekly housekeepers? Do you need a full blown television package when you can get by on free/inexpensive internet options? Do you really need that subscription radio service? Look for things/memberships you can cancel for the moment. It adds up. Many places will let you pause a membership for case such as these, without penalty. So ASK!

- Look for necessary expenditures that could be downgraded to save money (phone plans, deluxe garbage service, food/grocery delivery, etc.)

- Look up the people who owe you money and tell'em it's time to pay it back

- Want to hang out with friends but need to pull in the reins on spending? Game Nights are a great way to have a bunch of fun without spending money. Rotate at each others' places, and do the ole potluck & BYOBeverage thing. Low cost fun!

- Date Nights do not need to cost anything. Get creative and come up with fun things to do that are free, or are very close. These sorts changes may even stay with you long after you find a new job— saving you a lifetime of money!

- Got a life insurance policy by chance? Some people have policies that can be borrowed against. Not sure? Call and ask your agent.

9:30am TEMPORARY INCOME-Look for ways to bring in additional income. Make it a "game." This week your goal is to figure out how to legally make an extra $50 a day, next week $75 a day, or whatever your want your escalating goal to be. It gets the entrepreneurial juices flowing, and it helps you pay the bills and eat, so there's always that bonus, too. Anytime you do not have to tap into savings or a severance it is a good thing.

- Did you sign up for Unemployment? If not, do it NOW, if you've held a legit paying job before. It's not a guarantee, but nothing ventured, nothing gained

- Turn in your recycling for cash (if you can do that where you live)

- Check out what people are giving away on Craigslist, Marketplace, etc, that you could pick-up for free and turn around and sell

- Check out freelancing sites

- Check out Temp. Agency Sites

- Ask friends and family if they have some odd jobs you could do for them

- Are you in a position to rent out a room in your home? Can you possibly move somewhere temporarily & legally sublet your place?

- Look into working as a food delivery person, etc.

You get the picture. Another thing you could do is ask friends about unique side gig work they may know about. Ask, ask, ask! Don't be too proud. Think of it his way, if you can do some side work for friends or family, you could actually list them a reference and they could truly & honestly attest to what a great employee you are—so double win!!!

10:30 am TO DO LIST—Work on your other top priorities

12:30 pm LUNCHTIME-Take 30 and try to decompress

1:00 pm   30 MINUTE EMAIL CHECK

1:30 pm   NETWORKING

- Review your **NETWORKING/CONTACTS LIST** and determine who your Daily 3 are for the day and contact them (FOR TODAY, SEEK OUT 3 PEOPLE WHO YOU KNOW WHO MORE RECENTLY LANDED A NEW CAREER). Don't know anyone like that? Then be sure to ask your Daily 3 if they know anyone you could touch base with who has gone through a similar situation. Follow-up with those people right away). Comparing notes with others who have gone through a similar experience is a great way to learn from others' mistakes and their best practices; thus, saving you gobs of time!

- Next, get on Facebook and search special interest groups related to work/finding work and ask to join those groups.

- Finally, go to Meet-up.com and look for similar special interest groups and RSVP to attend a meeting. These don't have to be all professional, either. Joining large interest group meet-ups affords an opportunity to meet more people and network. Put those meetings on your calendar and be sure to go!

3:00 pm JOB SEARCHING

- Spend the rest of your "work day" searching for new jobs online. Be sure to check out the employment tabs on the internet for the companies you have listed on your **BUSINESS LIST** and the listings your

JOB SEARCH ENGINEs have sent you. (Basically, whenever you can set up job search engines to automatically send you listings do it! It will save lots of time).

4:45 pm ACCOUNTABILITY PARTNER-FIND ONE!

You may notice that you still have "Accountability Partner" on your TO DO List. Having an Accountability Partner is a great success strategy and can be used for all sorts of life goals. (Finding a new job, weight loss, fitness, project completion, etc.) When you know you need to answer to someone about your progress, you tend to hold yourself more accountable to make real progress—which often leads to greater success.

An Accountability Partner, in this case, is someone who you can count on to check in with you daily to see how you are doing, to inquire on your progress and daily accomplishments. Someone to share how your Daily 3 discussions went, to be a sounding board, etc. You need to select someone to be this person for you. (You may even want to ask him/her if they would like you to reciprocate on some sort of goal he/she is working on). WIN-WIN!

For me, this person was my significant other, and visa versa when he lost his job. Each day I would check with him on how things were going. I would ask him to share the highlights of his accomplishments with me. I'd ask him who his Daily 3 were and what transpired when he connected with them. I would ask if he added anything new to his Job Search List or Business List. You get the picture. As his Accountability Partner, I was the person he held himself "accountable to," because he knew each and every day I was going to ask for his recap of the day, and he knew he needed to have authentic stuff to report.

I still have Accountability Partners who I work with on a weekly basis, for various projects I am working on. We reciprocate by checking in on each other to see how each other's week is going, finding out what sort of progress we've each made and what the next steps are for the following week. We also are there to bounce ideas off each other. It is not a competition, it is a total circle of support. Even when we are working on our own projects, we keep each other in mind in the event we come across something that might benefit the other person. Together we are more successful, as a result of our weekly accountability check-ins.

5pm Get ready to call it a day!
Review today's accomplishments and tomorrow's To Do List.
Then, read **DAY 4: LET'S GET RESOURCEFUL.**
- Time to go do something fun or relaxing. Take the time to do this! It helps your brain have a break, and can often lead to great inspiration. You've worked hard today, so give yourself the evening off, or go meet up with some of those friends you've been meaning to get back to.

Get it? Got it? Good! Now that you understand the ins and outs of Day 3's To DOs, here's a simplified version of the schedule. You will need to start writing out your own schedule next week, but for now, I'm saving you time and helping you get used to the format, by doing it for you:

Day 3 Schedule:

7:00 am/or earlier-	**30+ minutes doctor-approved exercise**
7:30 am-	**Breakfast/Shower, etc**
8:00 am-	**Check your email (set your timer for 30 min.)**
8:30 am-	**DAILY AGENDA REVIEW/PRIORITY TASK TIME** (To Do List)

> Review yesterday's Accomplishments & Today's To Do List.
> Prioritize the To Do List and get at least the top three most important things on that list done before lunch today (which are the tasks added for today, refer to the guidebook for details)
> Remember to note Today's Accomplishments as you check off your To Do List

8:45am-	**Trim the Fat**
9:30am-	**Temporary Income**
10:30am-	**Other To Do List Tasks**--Work on your other top priorities now
12:30 pm-	**Lunchtime (Try to get in some sort of 10+ min movement)**
1:00 pm-	**Check your email (set your timer for 30 min.)**
1:30 pm-	**Networking Time (Daily 3)**

> (FOR TODAY, seek out 3 people who more recently landed a new career). Pay close attention to the other networking tasks to accomplish today, from the guidebook. These are very important strategies for 21st Century job searching

3:00pm-	**Job Searching**

Spend the rest of your "work day" searching for new jobs Online, using your Businesses/Job Search Engine Lists.

4:45pm-   **ACCOUNTABILITY PARTNER-**
                            Find one!

5:00pm-   **Get ready to call it a day.**

                            First, be sure you've written down all your Accomplishments

                            Second, transfer any TO DOs over to tomorrow's List

                            Third, read the guidebook's **DAY 4: LET'S GET RESOURCEFUL; (then go play)!**

DAY 4 PREP:
Here we go, this next part will get you ready for Day 4, so no time to waste, let's get right to it!

"A resourceful person will always make opportunity fit his or her needs."
~Napoleon Hill

Chapter 7
DAY 4: LET'S GET RESOURCEFUL

There are so many resources out there to help you along the way of getting back on track.

- One of the the things I highly recommend is making sure your library card is updated for your local library. There are many FREE reasons I mention this. First of all: audible books. I didn't have a coach to help me get going, it was all on me, but I did surround myself with many pseudo-literary coaches, if you will. I started "reading" every single business how-to book I could find through my local library. The beauty is, I was able to download and listen to these books everyday while I exercised, and again during my stretch breaks throughout the day. This helped me tremendously. Why? Because I was able to glean new strategies, techniques and insight from those who have already blazed a successful path in life. Most of all, instead of going to the dark side and letting my deep-seeded negative thoughts surface and hijack my day, I was listening to powerful and positive voices imparting their wisdom as I cycled & walked during my exercise sessions; thus, amping myself up with great endorphins and positivity from top to bottom. (Hey, don't knock it 'til you try it—it may work for you too)!

  I also highly recommend getting in touch with your local libraries because some often have information on workshops for adults trying to update their resumes or brushing up on their interview skills, etc. I cannot speak for all counties, but the one I live in has the hook-up on some inexpensive Adult Education classes to learn basic computer skills, social media skills, Excel, PowerPoint, etc. So if you are in need of learning some 21st Century Skills fast, check with your local library.

- Something that is very important for you to do is to go through your email. Look for positive remarks and recognitions from people about your performance. PRINT THESE OUT. This serves a few different purposes. First, it can help jog your memory on some of the projects, etc. you've worked on that you might be able to add to your resume. Second, it can help with examples to add to cover letters when applying for jobs. Third, it can remind you of people who you may be able to use as a reference or ask to write you a letter of recommendation. Of course there are many others good reasons to do this, but another important one is it feels good too!!! And we all need a little positive pump-up now and then—and NOW is definitely a good time! Right?

- Another area to check for chunks of awesomeness is on your evaluations if you've ever held another job. ALWAYS keep copies of these in a file at home (even better, scan them and send them to your personal email). Skim through those and be sure to add important highlights to your resume. (Most of all, making a list of these attributes will help boost your confidence, especially for the interview process, and keep your mind fresh on different things you do best).

- Along these lines, a dear friend reminded me that one of her tips is to go back through projects, etc. to review the financial impact (what you were able to help save or how much you were able to make for the company). If this applies to you, this also bodes well for talking points in both cover letters (when applicable) and definitely during interviews. If not. Always keep track of this for future reference

- When you are working through all these different areas, it may spark some other ideas for you to mine more golden nuggets of your personal achievements. So, be sure to keep a list of goals you have achieved. (The I TOTALLY ROCK List could help house these). Also, many areas of how you were able to solve problems may come to mind. Write those down. Again, these are often key points that you may need to reference shortly, so make a list in your notebook!

Something to learn from this is that if you haven't already, from here on out you need to be keeping a KUDOS file, both physically and electronically. Print out those pieces of positivity, and also be sure to forward copies to your personal email and store in a little file in the cloud. Just set up a little folder in your personal email and label it something fun, like: PICK-ME UPS, or IMSOAWESOME, or KUDOS2ME, or whatever floats your boat. Just be sure to do it, so you are never in a situation again where you are sifting through emails trying to find past made accolades.

So, for Day 4, add to your To Do List:

LOOK FOR POSITIVE COMMENTS, ACCOLADES, etc.

Ok, here we go, onward and upward for Day 4-
(Did you make your bed and exercise? And NO, I am not going
to let you off the hook on that!)

7:00 am/or earlier-	**30+ minutes doctor-approved exercise**
7:30 am-	**Breakfast/Shower, etc**
8:00 am-	**Check your email (set your 30 min. timer)**
8:30 am-	**DAILY AGENDA REVIEW/PRIORITY TASK TIME** (To Do List)

Review yesterday's journal of
accomplishments &
Today's To Do List.
Prioritize the To Do List (& always
notate today's accomplishments as
you complete them), with this new
addition on top:
**LOOK FOR POSITIVE
COMMENTS, ACCOLADES, etc.**

12:30 pm-	**LUNCHTIME**-Take 30 to eat & rejuvenate
1:00 pm-	**30 MINUTE EMAIL CHECK**
1:30 pm-	**NETWORKING**

Daily 3
Social Media
interest/networking groups
(Facebook, LinkedIn, Meet-up, etc.)

3:00 pm-	**JOB SEARCHING**

Review Business List and
continue searching for jobs on-line

4:30pm	**Accountability Partner Time** (you

may need to customize when
this happens, but be sure to squeeze
it in somehow)
Reciprocate for each other: what went
well today, tomorrow's goals/priorities,
next steps

5pm	**Get ready to call it a day.**

First, be sure you've written down all
your Accomplishments

Second, transfer any TO DOs over to tomorrow's List
Third, read **DAY 5: OUT OF THE BOX THINKING**
Fourth, (go play)!

(Did you notice the schedule is getting easier? It will continue to do so as you knock out more and more priority tasks. YAY)!

So today was all about being resourceful. Resources can come from all sorts of places and people. You never know when someone you meet is going to lead you to your next career adventure.

DAY 4 EXERCISES

LOOK FOR POSITIVES, POSITIVE COMMENTS, ACCOLADES, & OTHER SET YOURSELF UP FOR SUCCESS EXERCISES

There are so many resources out there to help you along the way of getting back on track. Surround yourself with success and positivity.

Books/podcasts/YouTube Videos: Make a list of the next 5 success books/podcasts/or videos you plan to listen to, watch (or actually read)!

1. _____

2. _____

3. _____

4. _____

5. _____

Where is your nearest local library?

_____

What is the library's phone number?

_____

Now call them and ask if they have any adult job search workshops/work skills enhancement workshops, etc. Do they know of any job search resources? Networking groups?

What was the name of the librarian you spoke to?

_____

NEXT: Scour your address books/email & phone contacts lists, and add these people to your Networking/Contacts List

How many people were you able to add to your Networking List from this exercise? _____

Scour your emails for positive comments from people, etc. If you don't have, be sure you always print these out in the future! Also, if you can't access, think back to times when you received KUDOs. What were they for? List the areas that people praised and thanked you for your help/talent/skills, etc.:

1. _____

2. _____

3. _____

4. _____

5. _____

Evaluation time! Find your past evaluations (if you have any), and go through them. List your top 5 glowing remarks about you below:

1. _____

2. _____

3. _____

4. _____

5. _____

Feeling awesome? You should!

    FINANCIAL IMPACT-Next, think about if there were times that you saved your previous employers money? Were you ever assigned to any projects? If so, what was the financial impact for the company, as a result of your hard work? Take a moment to think through those. Sometimes you may have been able to save a company time or manpower for a job; what financial amount did that equate to?

Write out your notes on this here:

GOALS ACHIEVED-List any newfound golden nuggets of your personal achievements you have discovered on your **I TOTALLY ROCK LIST** under **Strengths.** This helps serve as a central point of highlighted accomplishments that you may refer to when drafting a cover letter or prepping for a future meeting or interview.

Next, keep a list of goals you have achieved and/or any problems you were able to solve for your previous employers. Write those down on your Strengths List.(If you need to add an extra sheet or two in your notes for this, then bravo, go for it)!

Now that you have finished this, go back to your To Do List, to take care of your next set of priorities for the day.

DAY 5 PREP:
On day 5 we explore Out of the Box Thinking. By now, you should be putting together a solid schedule for yourself and seeing the benefits of hitting the various components. But today, I also want you to revisit your "**I TOTALLY ROCK LIST.**"

Take a look at the more "professional" skills you listed. Circle the top 5-6 that you just absolutely LOVE doing (or at least enjoy to a certain degree).

Now write them out here:

_____

_____

_____

_____

_____

_____

When looking at just this list, what sorts of jobs come to mind.
Pretend a friend with these skills above was asking you to
brainstorm what sort of jobs he/she could apply for with those skills.
What would you advise?   Write them down:

_____

_____

_____

_____

_____

_____

_____

_____

_____

_____

Ok, with this list of potential jobs, that utilizes skills that you enjoy, which industries employ people for these positions?   You may only think of one or two, but over the weeks to come, as you are reaching out to your Daily 3, ask each person their thoughts. You may discover an industry you never thought of before!

_____

_____

_____

_____

_____

_____

For each of these industries, take some time during your Businesses Lists part of your day and explore industry search engines.

Next, add to your To Do List for next Monday, to search the internet for some sites to explore industries. Vault.com as a great section, and so does the United States Department of Labor with their Occupational Outlook Handbook, and CareerOneStop has a bunch of great information for career comparisons, etc.

You should also look for sites that have career assessments. One of my favorites is MyNextMove.org. It has a great Interests assessment to get you started. BE HONEST when you complete the quiz. I really like their industry browse section, as well. I also use the key areas determined by the Interests assessment to plug in to their Search Careers section a and was surprised by the positions that utilize my interests.
Now that you are movin' and groovin', let's explore some Out of the Box Thinking tips in Chapter 8:

"Believe in yourself, listen to your gut, and do what you love."
~Dylan Lauren

Chapter 8
DAY 5: OUT OF THE BOX THINKING

Following are some suggestions for you to possibly try. These are a bit "out of the box," so some ideas may resonate with you, or maybe all, (or maybe none). The point is to get your creative juices flowing to help spark ideas of helping you to stand out in a crowd of applicants.

YOU SHOULD'VE BEEN IN PICTURES-One of my favorite "out of the box" tips was shared by a good friend when my husband lost his job. She mentioned she knows someone who puts together her own customized video presentations and sends them to companies she is interested in working for, without there even being a job posting. (Did you know most jobs that are available out there aren't even posted? Yup. That IS a shocker, so this is a great way to get your foot in the door.) This gal helps companies see why they need to create a position for her, and how she would be such an asset for their company.
'

PUT YOUR HEADS TOGETHER-Find one, two or three people who may be looking for work as well, or who may be considering a career change. Schedule a weekly "meeting of the minds" to discuss job searching aspects, resources, leads and whatnot. Maybe divide and conquer on reading business books, articles, etc. and have each person read a different one each week and present key points they learned from those books/articles at the next meeting. Regardless of your meeting agenda, be sure everyone stays on point, nobody monopolizes the whole meeting and that everyone walks away feeling like it was productive. Remember, this is a collaboration method. (Take this an extra step farther and possibly agree to also be each others' Accountability Partners).

TOOT YOUR OWN HORN-Create a very short video as a brief interview of yourself. Think of it as a "what you see is what you get" pitch of sorts that explains why you are an asset to an organization.

(This is different from the deliberate presentations mentioned above). Then upload this to YouTube, and add the link to your cover letters, and your resume. This is a unique way of allowing prospective employers a personal glimpse at who they would be interviewing. Keep in mind that you need to be professional, but not stiff and cold. Be warm, inviting and confidant. (Also be sure that you have a squeaky clean YouTube account)!

BE YOUR OWN MARKETING TEAM-Create an ad with a link to your personal professional website, highlighting yourself and your attributes, (as well as your resume). Then engage in strategic advertising via Social Media to target the industries you are trying to attract. Don't have a personal professional website? Most people don't, unless it is a blog. So develop one (not a blog, just a personal site). Or at minimum, create a page and publish to the web so that it can be accessed via link. A simple page with a brief bio and your resume will do.

FLIP YOUR PRESENCE AT JOB FAIRS-While Job Fairs are not "out of the box," finding a way for standing out at one definitely presents a challenge! Prospective employers establish a presence at these events, in order to do two things: 1) Meet a mass amount of people quickly who could be possible candidates for upcoming positions, and 2) Public Relations (making sure they are demonstrating they are a strong company that people should want to work for, etc.) So essentially, a Job Fair is a See & Be Seen event for all intensive purposes. That said, you need to attend these with the same mentality. So what is your plan of attack to get noticed and be remembered?

In addition to your resume, you should have some business cards printed up. There are online companies that can do this very inexpensively. (And they are very handy to keep on you at all times—you never know who you will run into, and where)! Be sure you choose a more unique style of card...but don't go dorky. Remember, this is a tool that is representing you! I recommend a couple things with style: If possible order a card with a non-traditional shape: square or maybe a circle. Also, you want the card to be a golden rod type color (red is also very noticeable—but can be a little "too in your face" depending on how it is designed).

On these business cards you should have a link to your personal (professional) website (for which you will already have your resume on), as well as the link to the video intro you made and put on YouTube. Splurge a bit and add a backside to your card that lists your greatest skill-set strengths. Make sure your font size is 12pt or larger to make it easier for others to read, and your name should be about 2 pts larger than whatever other size you make the rest of the text. When handing this card out, be sure to mention your name & be sure to mention your links on the card. (It's a memory thing, just go with it). At events like job fairs, you want to help the recruiters from the various businesses to remember you. So be sure to do a few more things to help them remember you and your name:

- Bring a name tag, just in case there aren't any. Whenever possible write your name in dark blue ink and use a red pen to make a box around your name. VERY IMPORTANT: Always wear your name tag on your right side. The reason is simple: people tend see it and remember it more because we tend to shake hands in our culture when meeting people, and we shake with our right hand. Therefore the eye tends to view to the right when shaking hands. (Great "ah ha moment" right? You're welcome!)

- While shaking hands, give a sincere compliment: "Hi! I am Michele Giacomini, it is very nice to meet you, and I just need to tell you (lean in slightly here) I have been admiring your earrings." (Or compliment a color they are wearing or their shoes, etc. but make sure you mean it). Even better, whenever possible, if you know something about that person, use a more personal compliment: "Hi! I am Michele Giacomini, and I am thrilled to meet you. I read your article on LinkedIn about (blah, blah, blah)."

- If you can get a conversation going, that could really work to your favor. Try to "naturally" find something you have in common and think of something (ie:. info on the topic you are discussing) you can offer to send the person at a later time, via email, or something that they could send you via email, etc. The thing is, you are trying to have an excuse to write something on your business card...because it gives the person another reason to remember you. Your excuse for writing on the card should be something like, "If you don't hear from me by Monday, please zip me an email." Hand it to the person and THEN say, "Even better, do you have a business card?" Most likely they do, so take it, and right in front of them, write on the card "Email (blah, blah, blah)." This will help you to remember who that person was when you are going through your cards later, and it gives you an opportunity to contact them again (and they are going to remember you, because they will recall you were going to email them about the blah, blah, blah you discussed).

- Another little tip is to wear something very unique. That doesn't mean wear a clown suit! Dress professionally, but wear an interesting brooch/lapel pin. Why? Because it may give the recruiter an opportunity to comment on it, thus, helping them to remember you even more! (And yes, wear it above your name tag. Just another strategy for the Name Game).

- After the Job Fair is over, make sure you take the time to send personalized thank you notes to the recruiters. (Hopefully you have that extra special something you promised to get back to them on, or you were going to check with them about). Regardless, take this opportunity to thank them for the time they spent chatting with you. You will want to reiterate your conversation, let them know that after much thought, you realized you walked away very interested in exploring opportunities for employment at their organization, and ask a question or two, in order to spur on-going communication.

If any of these Out of the Box techniques resonate with you, or help spark a different idea, be sure to write them down and add to your To Do List. If not, no worries, just let them marinate in the back of your mind. You may not follow of any of these, but the hope is that in the back of your mind, you begin brewing some unique ideas of your own!

Are you ready for Day 5? You should be! You are doing great. By now you've been putting one foot in front of the other. You are moving forward, despite any feelings you may have toward the worklife you just had yanked out from under you. SO BRAVO!!! Keep it up! And anytime you think you are not making progress, stop and get out your accomplishments journal and review the day or the week and see how much you have done. It's a lot more than you may be giving yourself credit for, so pat yourself on the back and keep on, keepin' on!

Now let's take Day 5 by storm: (You've got this. And YES, I know you made your bed and exercised already—so I am not going to even ask, because I trust you)!

7:00 am/or earlier-	**30+ minutes doctor-approved exercise**
7:30 am-	**Breakfast/Shower, etc**
8:00 am-	**Check your email (set your 30 min. timer)**
8:30 am-	**DAILY AGENDA REVIEW/PRIORITY TASK TIME** (To Do List) (Remember, worst for first)! Today, for your Top Priority, add **Day 5 OUT OF THE BOX THINKING EXERCISES**. Then do them, and then return to your other top priorities.
12:30 pm-	**LUNCHTIME**-Take 30 min. to eat & rejuvenate
1:00 pm-	**30 MINUTE EMAIL CHECK**
1:30 pm-	**NETWORKING** Daily 3 Social Media interest/ networking groups (Facebook, LinkedIn, Meet-up. etc.)
3:00 pm	**JOB SEARCHING** Review Business List and continue searching & APPLYING for jobs on-line
4:30 pm	**Accountability Partner Time** Reciprocate for each other: what went well today, tomorrow's goals/priorities, next steps
5:00 pm	**Get ready to call it a day.** **First,** be sure you've written down all your Accomplishments **Second**, transfer any TO DOs over to tomorrow's List **Third** (go play)! (Reading the last of this book is a great option, or save it for tomorrow, your choice)

With "out of the box thinking" comes a chance to meet others who have found a way to make a living, and for some, much different than they intended! Be sure to talk to people about their journey. Discuss with store owners how they started their businesses, ask successful friends about their paths. You will probably discover that all the paths taken had their struggles, but by seeking out these people and learning from them, and the risks they took, you may find yourself very inspired!

Max

Max didn't know what to expect when he decided to create his own safety net of job security. He was working for a company that suddenly found themselves failing at a rapid rate, after 60 years of business. Max knew it was time to get a side hustle going, and fast!

Luckily, Max had many years of pool building experience from his years before entering corporate America. So he and his wife decided to go for it.

"Owning my own business was scary at first. You don't 'know' if it will succeed and there is a ton of pressure on you to make it happen," shares Max. "My wife was the biggest support and I couldn't do it without her. My new career path aligns more with my life goals than corporate America did. Freedom to spend more time with family (kinda ha,ha), set my own schedule, and of course financially it has been an improvement. It also opens up other business opportunities."

So knowing that they were jumping into this adventure together, helped Max with the support he needed, which built his confidence, as well.

"The goal of my business was a 'side business,' but also a safety net to fall back on." Max says that if you are going to build a business, there are some things you should consider, as he has learned first hand that safety nets are critical. "If you have a skill or special training use that to your advantage. If you don't have a safety net or side business I think it's helpful to at least have an eye out for job opportunities and understand industry trends. I saw the warning signs in (my former) industry and it forced me to

---

create that backup plan."He shared that by being proactive, it spared him from the typical "lay off situations" where he would have been put out and just have to believe everything will be okay.

Now his side business has become a quickly growing full-time business and he and his wife could not be happier, nor prouder!

Max exclaims, "We are very excited to see what other great adventures await us. Now that I own a business I am continually thinking of ways to diversify."

You aren't quite done yet...keep going for a little more on Day 5!

LESSON: DAY 5

DAY 5 OUT OF THE BOX THINKING EXERCISES:

List 5 companies you could send a video resume to:

1. _____

2. _____

3. _____

4. _____

5. _____

List 3-5 people to start weekly Meeting of the Minds Networking Group with:

1. _____

2. _____

3. _____

4. _____

5. _____

Write out your 30 second personal commercial/"Elevator Speech":

GET CREATIVE! Now create a video of you delivering your 30 second personal commercial speech. What more would you need to do to polish that up and upload to YouTube?

Next, take a few minutes to look at Blogger or other Blogging sites. What would it take to upload your resume there and and add a brief bio, and maybe the video bio that your recorded? Add your notes on this here:

LIST 5 UPCOMING JOB FAIRS:

1. _____

2. _____

3. _____

4. _____

5. _____

Now add each of those to your calendar and your TO DO List. BE SURE TO ATTEND!

List YOUR own Out of the Box ideas here: (Remember, nothing is too crazy, as long as it is legal, right?) GO FOR IT, this is a safe zone for your thoughts and dreams!

So at this point, you are finished with the "boot camp" part of the guidebook. You've gotten organized, you've gathered the parts and pieces of the what you need to move toward finding your next job. But I just can't leaving you there, because I've got a few more tips for you to keep you going. So take a moment to read the last two chapters of the guidebook now.

"Ambition is the first step to success.
The second step is action."
~Author unknown

Chapter 9
NOW WHAT?

So it's been a week and you've dealt with a lot! Possibly all sorts of emotions, possibly lots of conversations with a multitude of people all about the same thing, wading through the fog and figuring out your next steps. But with all that and more, you've kept in motion. Instead of spending a week doing nothing but feeling sorry for yourself, you've been proactive, you've gotten yourself on track and you are now in the routine of your new job of Finding a New Job. You may be starting to apply for positions, and with that means you may be interviewing soon. You may be starting to meet with friends and connections to discuss job leads and opportunities. All of it can be very overwhelming and scary and exciting and all of the above, all at once! That's just part of this adventure. (The bright sides)!!!

Some days your routine will need to adjust a bit to accommodate meetings, etc. That's okay! Just be sure stick with the routine, even if it is an abbreviated day. Some people have asked me how to do that once they are going out on interviews, etc. They also want to know how to keep up with it when they've been forced to take a position that they only plan to keep for temporary. My advice is to simply do what works for you, but keep doing it!

ABBREVIATED DAY: GREAT THINGS COME IN SMALL PACKAGES

For me, my abbreviated days looked something like:

30 MINUTE-EXERCISE

DAILY AGENDA—Review & Prioritize top 2 tasks for To Do List

30 MINUTE-EMAIL CHECK

2 HOURS-PRIORITY TASK TIME (Remember, worst for first)!

30 MINUTES-DAILY 3

1 HOUR-JOB SEARCHING

(If I could fit in more later in the day, great, if not, I was sure to write in ALL CAPS on my accomplishments for the day that I had an INTERVIEW or CONFERENCE/LUNCH MEETING w SO & SO). Those are time consuming, but necessary, and very big deals. So they are always worth an abbreviated day!

KEEPING YOUR OPTIONS OPEN

This is going to sound horrible, but take it in first before passing judgment, and remember that this is coming from years of experience. I have learned the hard way that being loyal to a company should never be your priority. Businesses and organizations are not typically loyal to their employees. A friend of mine said it best when she shared a thought from her father. He told her that no employee is a permanent one. We are all really temporary in some way, shape or form from Day 1. Do NOT get me wrong. This is not an excuse to suddenly become a slacker, with lack of work ethic and develop a total disregard for having pride in a job well done. It simply means, if the grass is greener somewhere else, then maybe you need to graze in lusher pastures. Always look out for YOU! Have your own back, because there are NO guarantees that any organization is going to watch it for you. Most are looking out for their bottom dollar and will can anyone's ass to save their own. Just saying. So from here on out, always keep your options open.

You can do this by keeping a "Maintenance Schedule" whether you have a job and you are looking for a career change, or if you simply took on a job somewhere to pay the bills. Simply, designate a minimum of 2-3 days/evenings per week, (maybe even while sitting in front of the tv, if it's not too distracting), to follow this ultra abbreviated schedule. It's extra condensed, because you need to keep up the hobby/interests at least 2-3 days per week, for life. (I mean, you know what they say, "All work and no play…," right?)

Please note, one thing that transitions is your Daily 3 now becomes your Weekly 3, BUT you need to actually talk to them. Put your Hands-free to use and call them while you are sitting in traffic, or while you walk the dog. But calendar and call. (One tip I like is to make sure all these people who you've recently reconnected with, stay connected, by putting them on your To DO List for their birthday, and every three months from there on out). Staying connected is how we continue to stay fresh on people's minds & visa versa! Seriously, we may need their help now, but they may need us later. (And it always feels good to help others by giving back and by paying it forward).

MAINTENANCE SCHEDULE: 2-3 Days Per Week

Review Agenda & Prioritize To Do List
30-60 MINUTES-TO DO LIST (Knock off 1 or 2 items—priorities first)!
30 MINUTES-WEEKLY 3 (a minimum of one person each day that you connect with)
30 MINUTES-JOB SEARCH
30 MINUTES-EMAIL CHECK

LESSON: Now what?

Well, when you've gotten this far, it is time to pat yourself on the back. Remember, you will only get as much out of this program as your put in. It's time to reflect. If this is your first week with this program, then it was a hard one. If it is week 2 or more, then you probably have seen some customizations to the routine evolve. You've been customizing your To Do Lists, and over time there will be less and less of the Finding It TO DOs, and more and more of your own that naturally come up as you work through your routine each day.

If ever you you feel yourself spiraling, start back on the program with a quick review of Day 1 and work through the schedule of Days 2, 3, 4 & 5, (and follow it diligently)! This will help you reset and get back on track with focus and productivity.

REFLECTION: I recommend taking time out at the end of each week to reflection on your progress. If you are finishing the first week of this program, definitely stop and reflect in the **NOTES:** section of your Daily Journal (or in this workbook). Write as much as you want--some weeks you may write just a little, other weeks you may find yourself pouring out tons of thoughts...there is no word count minimum or maximum, so just do it. (And I highly recommend continuing this practice once you find your new job. It will host a lot of great information for you as resource, while you always keep your options open)!

- What do I now understand more clearly about my "WHY?"
- How clearly do I understand my goal? Do I need to tweak it or is it good as it is?
- What were my biggest discoveries this week?
- What were my biggest "AH HA!" moments?
- What are my top 5 accomplishment this week I'm most proud of?
- What are my goals that I want to conquer next week?
- How am I different today, than I was the day before I started the Finding It program?
- How can I help others get through a tough time like this?

WEEK 1 WRAP-UP (REFLECTION)

What do I now understand more clearly about my "WHY?"

How clearly do I understand my goal? Do I need to tweak it or is it good as it is?

What were my biggest discoveries this week?

What were my biggest "AH HA!" moments?

What are my top 5 accomplishments this week I'm most proud of?

What are my goals that I want to conquer next week?

How am I different today, than I was the day before I started the Finding It program?

How can I help others get through a tough time like this?

WEEK 2 WRAP-UP (REFLECTION)

What do I now understand more clearly about my "WHY?"

How clearly do I understand my goal? Do I need to tweak it or is it good as it is?

What were my biggest discoveries this week?

What were my biggest "AH HA!" moments?

What are my top 5 accomplishments this week I'm most proud of?

What are my goals that I want to conquer next week?

How am I different today, than I was the day before I started the Finding It program?

How can I help others get through a tough time like this?

WEEK 3 WRAP-UP (REFLECTION)

What do I now understand more clearly about my "WHY?"

How clearly do I understand my goal? Do I need to tweak it or is it good as it is?

What were my biggest discoveries this week?

What were my biggest "AH HA!" moments?

What are my top 5 accomplishments this week I'm most proud of?

What are my goals that I want to conquer next week?

How am I different today, than I was the day before I started the Finding It program?

How can I help others get through a tough time like this?

WEEK 4 WRAP-UP (REFLECTION)

What do I now understand more clearly about my "WHY?"

How clearly do I understand my goal? Do I need to tweak it or is it good as it is?

What were my biggest discoveries this week?

What were my biggest "AH HA!" moments?

What are my top 5 accomplishments this week I'm most proud of?

What are my goals that I want to conquer next week?

How am I different today, than I was the day before I started the Finding It program?

How can I help others get through a tough time like this?

"I find the best way to help someone is not to change them, but instead, help them to reveal the greatest version of themselves."
~Dr. Steve Maraboli

Chapter 10
YOUR LOVED ONES NEED SUPPORT TOO!

This chapter is a special note for the "Support System" of the person who is job seeking: **(So show it to your support people. The sooner in the the process, the better.)** Seriously, help them, to help you. Even better, encourage them to read the whole book! Please keep in mind, sometimes it is hard for your loved ones to 1) Wrap their minds around what is happening to you, and 2) You are changing your habits to be productive and successful, and sometimes that is also hard for some to understand.

I truly believe allowing them to read about the transformations you are going through so you may kick some booty on this job search process, will really help them see the whole picture.

What many people tend to forget is that when someone is jobless, oftentimes it brings on great stress to others as well. When my husband was laid off, we suddenly lost close to 66% of our income. OUCH! He had been our financial rock of the family. He had always encouraged me to do what I wanted with my career, because he could take care of us. Then that horrible day came when my rock was rocked. It was now up to me, solely, to keep us going. After almost 30 years of marriage, I was now the sole breadwinner for our family. (Secretly, I had always dreamed of making more money than my husband—but this was certainly NOT the way I wanted to do it)!

When I was in my early 20s, there were a couple of times I had humble myself and move home to save money. This was hard on me, and also my parents, who now had an extra person running up utility bills, feeling like they needed to feed, etc.

I mention this, because you may now be in the same position as the support to someone who is jobless, and now need to be the sole provider, (while simultaneously needing to support that loved one who is dazed and confused and trying to find his/her way toward new/first employment). But the reality is, there is some serious disbelief and despair YOU are probably going through, as well. I get it. It's awful to feel and it is awful to watch. Furthermore, there is no crystal ball to help you see that all will be okay, (and more importantly, when)!

Everyone is different on how they handle this. You can bury your head in the sand & pray this isn't happening, (but we both know that won't get you anywhere). OR! You could become super proactive.

- You can become the best cheerleader in the world and be the positive beacon in his/her life.

- You can become the ultimate pinnacle of resource for that person.

- You can become the networking guru of the universe and help make connections like crazy.

Whatever it is, when you find your way offering supporting, with the level of support that suits you both, you may also find yourself coping with this awful thing that has happened (to you too).

Here are a few tips for you on how to be a great support person:

1) Be sure you take care of yourself! Get doctor-approved exercise in everyday. You need to stay healthy through this process too! This is a stressful time, so give yourself permission to de-stress!
2) Read this book so you understand the process of the program that your loved one is trying to adapt to. It's hard,

and the first week is the hardest. It will get easier, for both of you. Just trust that in order to move forward, your loved one needs to put all the moving pieces in place and <u>stay in motion</u>.

3) Become a positive Accountability Partner. (NOT A NAG)! There is a difference!
   a) Do daily check-ins (at first—as weeks go by, every couple of days or so will suffice)
   b) Ask about his/her top accomplishments of the day
   c) Ask how the To Do List is going, and what are his/her next steps for the following day
   d) Ask who his/her Daily 3 was for the day
   e) Ask about the positive things he/she is discovering through this process
4) Help connect with YOUR resources. Ask people about leads, etc. then connect your loved one with those resources/people.
5) Share interesting articles, info., etc. in a kind, compassionate & respectful manner.
6) Establish times to connect and share each other's feelings. (Yes, that means YOU need to share your fears, concerns, etc. too)!
7) Be there.

You got this!

For additional success coaching services, contact us at:
www.TheDragonflyRanch.com

For specific coaching areas:
https://www.thedragonflyranch.com/business-coaching

For upcoming workshops, speaking events, and webinars:
https://www.thedragonflyranch.com/new-services

Author's Note:

I hope this book has been able to guide you through the crazy chaos you may have been going through before getting organized and helped you to get on track to looking for a new/first job or career. Be productive, be positive, & be persistent through this adventure. Life has a peculiar way of leading us to new discoveries, and this is one of the many in your life.

Wishing you well and encouraging you to keep at it, and remember, if life shuts a door in your face, frickin' kick it down and find your own new window of opportunity!

YOU GOT THIS!

About the author

O. Michele Giacomini is a writer, educator, and a promoter of others. With over 14 years of business experience, PLUS, over 19 years working in the education industry & professional development, she has much to contribute to help bolster the success of others. When she isn't writing for a variety of publications, as well as her humorous Miss OMG books, you can find her coaching others for success in careers, business, writing/publishing and organizational strategies—or tending to her chickens on the country property she shares with her husband, in Northern California.

You can follow her on Facebook at:
https://www.facebook.com/TheDragonflyRanch/

and/or:
https://www.facebook.com/groups/springboardtosuccess/

Or follow her on LinkedIn:
O. Michele Giacomini

_____

Other books by O. Michele Giacomini:

Looking for B.O.B. (BrightSides of Bull$#!+): Every Day
https://www.amazon.com/dp/153085721X

Surviving the Holidays: HELL-i-DAZE
https://www.amazon.com/dp/0578438399

Blindsided: Your One Week Guide Towards Finding it after you've Lost It
https://www.amazon.com/dp/0578489856

* 9 7 8 0 5 7 8 5 0 4 4 1 4 *